ADHD Does Not Have Me!

Attention Deficit Hyperactivity Disorder Explained by a Child

Desiree Corley Jones, LMHC

Text copyright © 2023 by Desiree Corley Jones
Illustrated by Reeha Zulfiqar
Produced by Adrienne Hand Editing
Book Design by Kaitlin Barry
Printed in the United States of America
All rights reserved
ISBN: 979-8-218-18857-3

Published by Step-By-Step 4 Help Foundation, Inc.
Jacksonville, Florida
https://www.step-by-step4help.com/

Dedicated to
my three children, Te'Jayah, Thomas, and Kevin, who
inspire me and make me so proud.
Always be the best that you can be.
~Mommy

Endorsements

If you want to help your child deal with ADHD, this is a fantastic book, and it will help! It will give children, teachers, and families an understanding of how a child can think positively and be successful with ADHD. I love this book!

~Dr. Sabrina Mixson, Executive Director of Compliance & Operations, Workforce Education Florida State College at Jacksonville

This book shows a positive image of a little girl with ADHD. It displays her having a positive attitude while dealing with ADHD. Cute, simple, and informative. This book is a must for a counselor's library!

~Shakesha Swift, Guidance Counselor, Duval County Public Schools

This is a great read-aloud book for children with ADHD. It shows they can keep calm and cool while dealing with ADHD in school. I encourage all schools to use this for their students to help them remain positive and succeed with ADHD.

~Cameron Frazier, Founder and Principal, Becoming Collegiate Academy

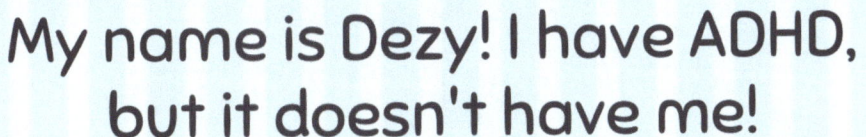

My name is Dezy! I have ADHD, but it doesn't have me!

I can do all things big and small.
I can even plant a tree.

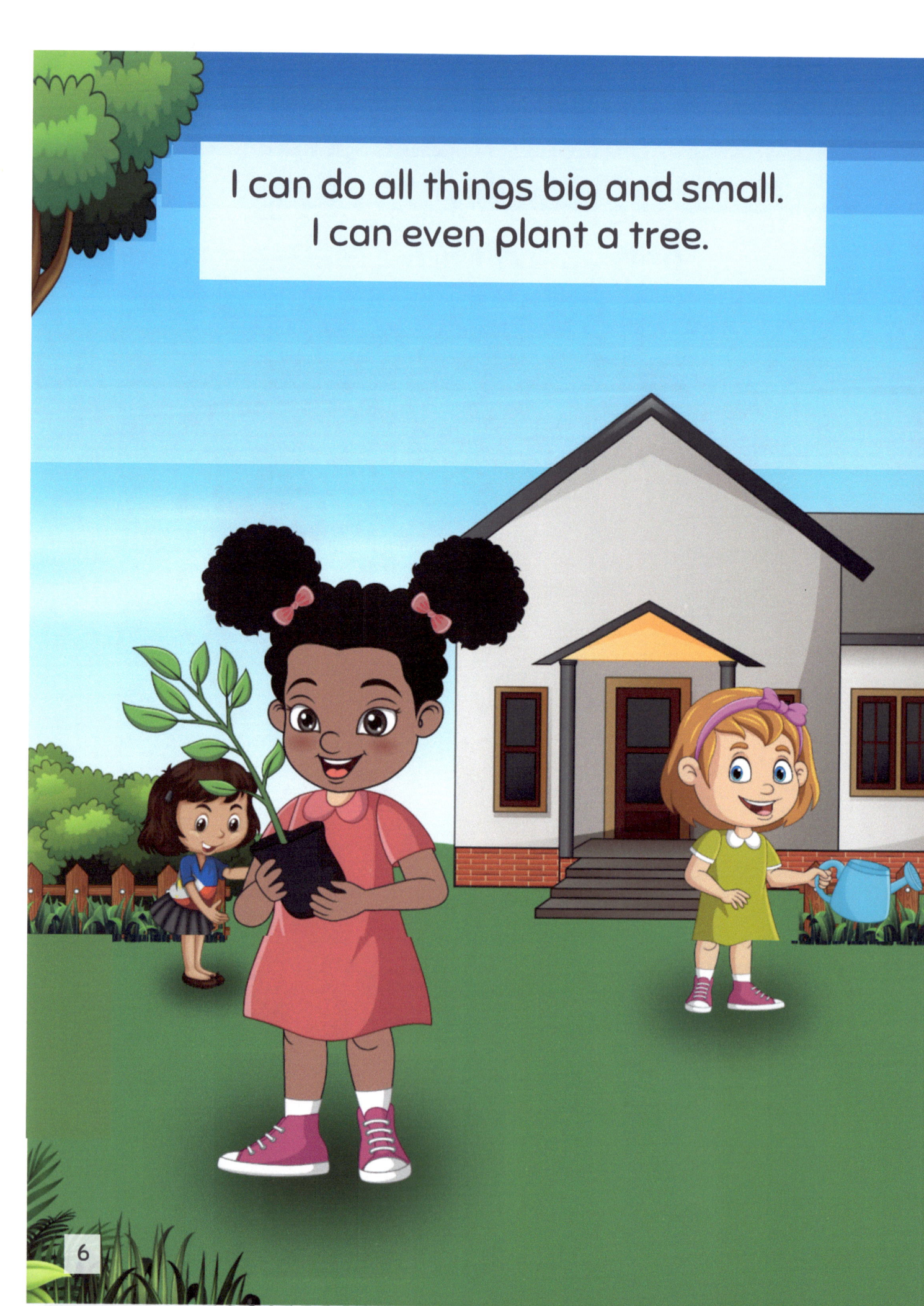

I help my family and friends, and they help me!

I love sports and math and science and when my friends play with me!

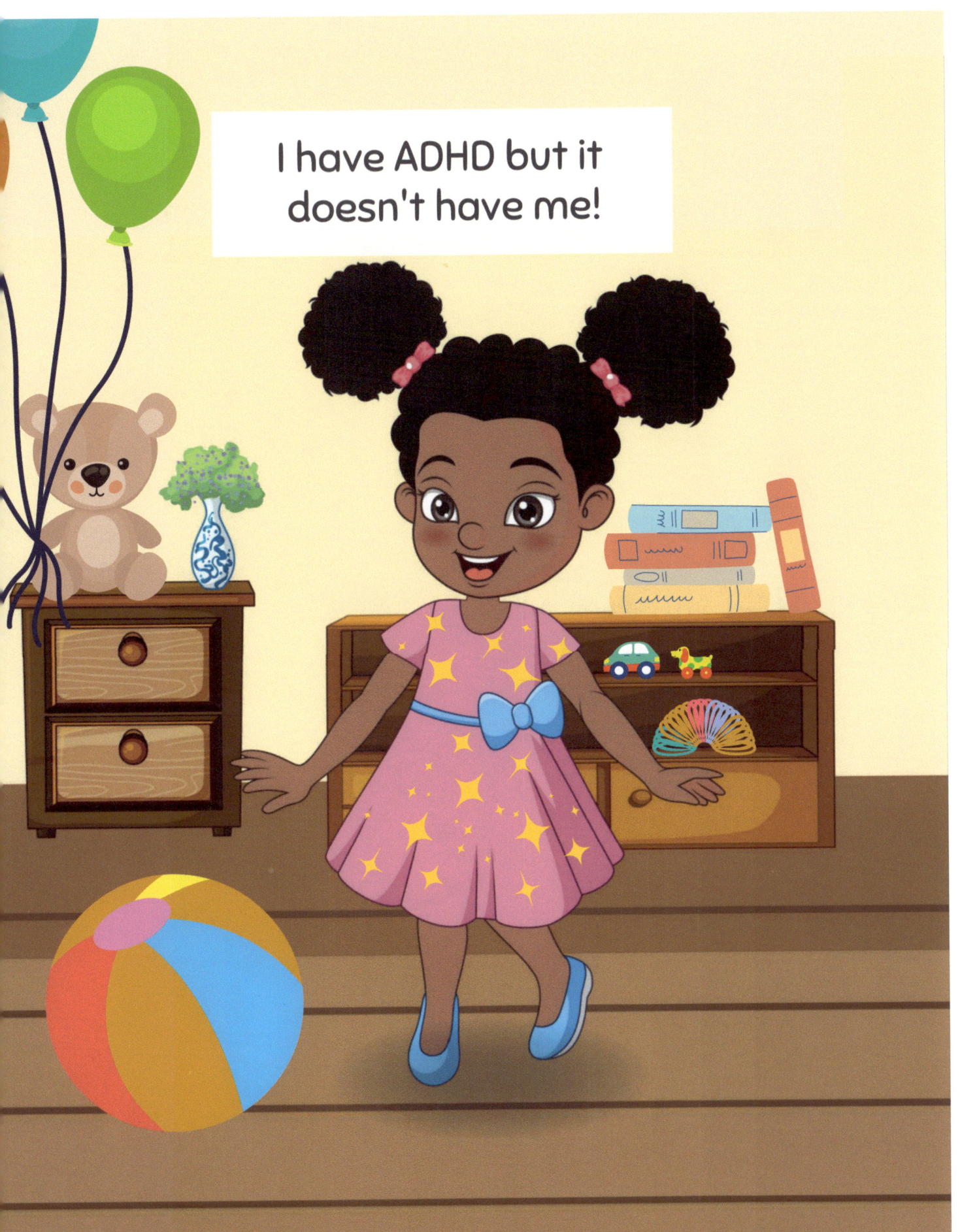

I have ADHD but it doesn't have me!

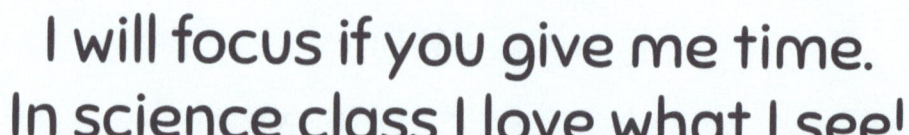

I will focus if you give me time.
In science class I love what I see!

$E = m.c^2$

$$x = \frac{-b \pm \sqrt{b^2 - 4ac}}{2a}$$

I need patience and a listening ear. So please, be kind when I'm near.

I don't always get it right,
but I always try!

I make mistakes but I won't give up even when times get tough.

Some don't understand when I forget things, talk out loud, and can't sit still. Please give me time to focus, and I will!

Kids may laugh and tease me,
but I know just what to do...

My therapist taught me how to keep calm and cool.

I take deep breaths and count to 10.
I say, Dezy, you can do anything!

I work hard to practice every day.
And every day I go outside and play!

My heart is full of dreams
and things I know I can do.
I can bake a cake – and so can you!

I have gifts and talents that
the world has to see!
Because ADHD does not have me!

Some people think I'm different and that's okay.

Kids may call me names
but I smile and pray.

I can do many things
and be anything I want to be!

Because I know ADHD <u>DOES</u> <u>NOT</u> have me!

Words I say every day!

I CAN DO WHATEVER I PUT MY MIND TO

I BELIEVE IN MYSELF

I AM PERFECT JUST THE WAY I AM

I AM CREATIVE

I AM LOVED

I LOVE MYSELF

I CAN WORK WITH MY ADHD

I HAVE A CLEAR MIND

Attention Deficit Hyperactivity Disorder
Daily Affirmations for Children

About the Author

Desiree Corley Jones is the Owner and Chief Executive Officer of both Step-by-Step Behavioral Health Services, and Step-by-Step 4 Help Foundation, Inc., as well as a licensed mental health counselor. She lives in Jacksonville, Florida with her husband, daughter, twin boys, and their dogs.

Desiree is a proud graduate of William M. Raines High School, Bethune Cookman College, and Webster University. A member of Delta Sigma Theta Sorority, Inc., she was awarded the 2023 JAX Chamber of Commerce Small Business Leader of the Year for the Three Rivers Council. Desiree was also awarded the Best Boss Award for the Best Non-Profit and Best Healthcare Services (2021), and the News 4 JAX The One to Watch Award. In 2016, she was a Child Abuse Prevention Honoree.

Inspired by helping others realize and reach their fullest potential, Desiree strives every day to make a difference in people's lives while bringing awareness to mental health. If you can heal from your trauma, and tap into your passion, you can "Make Your Pain Pay You!"

Her heroes and mentors include her sisters Arellia Corley and Shakesha Swift. "They have hearts of gold and inspire me to keep pushing during all adversity," she says. "They have strength and resilience like no other. They taught me to act without fear and love without limits. They are always right by my side in good and bad times and have unconditional love and support for me, my family, and all that I do."

An inspiration Desiree lives by
"You don't have to see the whole staircase, just take the First Step."
- Dr. Martin Luther King Jr.

Advocacy for Healthy Mental Living For All

In the US, only 20% of children with mental, emotional, learning, or behavioral disorders receive care from a specialized mental healthcare provider. Many families have to travel long distances or be placed on long waiting lists to receive care. Other obstacles include affordability, lack of internet and/or transportation, social stigma, and misinformation.

Our children deserve better.

In 2008, Desiree Corley Jones founded Step-by-Step 4 Help Foundation, Inc. in Jacksonville, FL, and in 2016 she founded Step-By-Step Behavioral Health Services in Gainesville, FL to strengthen and empower children, families, communities, and schools.

The mission of the Foundation is to reduce the stigma related to mental illness, intensify parental engagement, and reduce crime to create safer communities.

The mission of Step-by-Step Behavioral Services is to improve the lives of children and their families, and to assist them in reaching their fullest potential, guiding them step-by-step. Licensed, trained counselors provide integrated, quality, compassionate mental health treatment and services that support social-emotional wellness and growth.

Step-by-Step Behavioral Services include outpatient psychiatric services, psychosocial rehabilitation, community support, individual and family therapy, therapeutic behavioral on-site therapy, and mental health training in Gainesville and Jacksonville, Florida.

"We envision a world in which all people have access to information and treatment that can help them improve their mental, behavioral, and emotional health, and achieve harmony, thus promoting healthier families, schools, and communities."
~Desiree

Upcoming books by Desiree Corley Jones

ADHD Does Not Have Me! Workbooks

Bipolar Disorder Does Not Have Me! Book and Workbooks

Depression Does Not Have Me! Book and Workbooks

Anxiety Does Not Have Me! Book and Workbooks

Trauma Does Not Have Me! Book and Workbooks

ADHD and Mental Health Resources for teachers and parents

Children and Adults with Attention-Deficit/Hyperactivity Disorder (CHADD) is a national organization providing support, education, advocacy, and encouragement to parents, educators, and professionals. (chadd.org)

Teacher-to-Teacher is a teacher-designed interactive course for teachers who have children with ADHD in their classrooms.

Parent-to-Parent is an online course with short video lessons about ADHD and downloadable resources for parents who have children with ADHD. The program is also available in Spanish, free of charge.

National Resource Center on ADHD (NRC) works with CHADD to offer the latest evidence-based information on ADHD including helpful Fact Sheets that can be downloaded from the website.

The Child Mind Institute advances children's mental health by providing evidence-based care, delivering educational resources, training educators in underserved communities, and developing breakthrough treatments.

American Academy of Child and Adolescent Psychiatry (AACAP)

IDEA vs Section 504 school accommodations